GREEN CARD

JoAnne Akalaitis

BROADWAY PLAY PUBLISHING INC
New York
www.broadwayplaypublishing.com
info@broadwayplaypublishing.com

GREEN CARD
© Copyright 1991 JoAnne Akalaitis

All rights reserved. This work is fully protected under the copyright laws of the United States of America. No part of this publication may be photocopied, reproduced, stored in a retrieval system, or transmitted, in any form or by any means, electronic, mechanical, recording, or otherwise, without the prior permission of the publisher. Additional copies of this play are available from the publisher.

Written permission is required for live performance of any sort. This includes readings, cuttings, scenes, and excerpts. For amateur and stock performances, please contact Sarah L Douglas, Abrams Artists Agency (incorporating Flora Roberts, Inc), 275 7th Ave, 26th fl, NY NY 10001, 646 461-9376, sdouglas@dandkartists.com.

Cover art from the Mark Taper Forum production program

First edition: March 1991
This edition: May 2017
I S B N: 978-0-88145-082-8

Book design: Marie Donovan
Word processing: WordMarc Composer Plus
Typographic controls: Xerox Ventura Publisher, Professional Extension
Typeface: Palatino

GREEN CARD was originally produced by Center Theater Group of Los Angeles at the Mark Taper Forum, Gordon Davidson, Artistic Director, William P Wingate, Managing Director.

GREEN CARD was subsequently produced at the Joyce Theater as part of the First New York International Festival of the Arts. It opened on 13 June 1988, with the following ensemble and creative contributors:

Abraham Alvarez, Raye Birk, Jesse Borrego, Rosalind Chao, Pamela Dunlap, George Galvan, Jim Ishida, Josie Kim, Dana Lee, Alma Martinez, and Jessie Nelson.

Director	JoAnne Akalaitis
Set design	Douglas Stein
Costume design	Marianne Elliot
Lighting design	Frances Aronson
Choreography	Carolyn Dyer
Sound design	Jon Gottlieb
Projection design	Craig Collins

"America is not a nation so much as a world."
Herman Manville

CHARACTERS

RAYE, an Anglo man, 40-60 years old
JESSE, a young Latin man
ROSALIND, a young Asian woman
GEORGE, a Latin man, 20-40 years old
ABE, a Latin man in his 40s
JIM, an Asian man in his 40s
DANA, an Asian man, 30-50 years old
ALMA, a Latin woman, 20-40 years old
JESSICA, an Anglo woman, 20-40 years old
JOSIE, an Asian woman in her 20s
PAMELA, an Anglo woman, 35-50 years old

These characters are named after the actors who performed in the production at the Joyce Theater in New York in June 1988. The names and number of the performers can be changed to meet the needs of the director and the producer.

PROLOGUE

(Two women rush by. Scrim in.)

JESSICA: He said he wanted different things from life.

PAMELA: Like what?

JESSICA: These Perry Ellis tights make my legs look fat.

PAMELA: I'm starting regression therapy with this new guy next week.

JESSICA: I can't believe she's having an affair with her channeler.

(Music: Frank Sinatra's "The House I Live In")

(Slides of faces of immigrants from the 19th century)

(JOSIE has been asleep on the floor, wrapped in an American flag. She stands on a chair to speak.)

JOSIE: Not like the Brazen Giant of
Greek fame
With conquering limbs astride
from land to land,
Here at our sea-washed, sunset
gates shall stand
A mighty woman with a torch,
whose flame
Is the imprisoned lightning,
and her name
Mother of Exiles, from her
beacon hand
Glows worldwide welcome; her

mild eyes command
The air-bridged harbor that
twin cities frame....

"Keep ancient lands, your
stored pomp!"

Cries she
With silent lips, "Give me
your tired, your poor,
Your huddled masses yearning
to breathe free.
The wretched refuse of your
teeming shores.
Send these, the homeless,
tempest-tossed to me.
I lift my lamp beside the
Golden Door."

ACT ONE

JESSE: *(Rushes onstage with a hand mike, interrrupting the end of* JOSIE's *speech)* Are there any niggers here tonight? I know that's one nigger who works here. I see him back there. Oh, there's two niggers, customers, and ah, aha! Between those two niggers sits one kike. Man, thank God for the kike! *(He moves into the house during the speech)*

Uh, two kikes. That's two kikes, and three niggers, and one spic. One spic, two, three spics. One mick, one spic, one hick, thick, funky spunky boogie. And there's another kike...three kikes. Three kikes, one guinea, one greaseball. Three greaseballs, two guineas. Two guineas, one hunky funky lace-curtain Irish mick. That mick spic hunky funky boogie.

Two guineas plus three greaseballs and four boogies make three spics. Minus two yid spic Polack funky spunky Polacks. Five more niggers, give me five more niggers.

I pass with six niggers and eight micks and four spics.

Sold in America!

L. A. WOMAN

(Projections change to:)

DOWNTOWN
BEACH
HEALTH FOOD

NEW WORLD
GOLDEN L...
KNOW NOTHING

SEARS
MEL...G P...T

SALAD BAR
HE...TH F...D

VAL...T P...ARKING

LEGAL AID
VELVEETA
SUNTAN

NEW WAVE
SURFER
7-11

PA...KING LOT
SANDWICH BAGS
1-HR DRY CLEANING

(While projections are being shown, we hear:)

(Music: The Doors' "L.A. Woman", *very loud. The company moves in a tight little dance across the stage from left to right. At a slower moment in the music, each actor goes to a preset bundle and carefully unpacks and puts on classic Eastern European clothes—oversized overcoats, dark hats, long skirts and babushkas, and Ellis Island tags. The actors gather up their belongings, go to the long*

ACT ONE   5

benches upstage and obsessively tap out The Doors'
rhythm. Jewish Man (RAYE) has remained center stage.
He puts on a yarmulke and a shawl. He sits and waits.
As the song builds in volume and intensity, his frustration
grows.)

SUCCESS STORY

(Note: All the taped voices are from interviews.)

RAYE: *(He speaks with a warm, near-clichéd Jewish accent.)* Enough! Enough! Enough with the mojo! I was born in Lithuania when it was a province of the Czarist empire. It was such a tiny little town...it is probably not even on the map. There was a Christian church right in the middle of this town and when the church bells rang, we Jewish children would listen with childish wonder. On certain Christian festivals, they would have pageants coming from the church led by priests with colorful robes with crosses. Oh—we had our religious celebrations, too. My favorite was Pesach. Oh—how my mother would clean and scrub the house. A special man would come with a horse and carriage to deliver eggs and matzos to our house...and it was spring. *(Pause)*

(The entire group on benches assumes a very stylized freeze, reinforcing the story. It is abstract and sculptural. This mode is repeated throughout the story. Otherwise, they listen and watch, as if at a movie.)

RAYE: You heard about the pogroms? The goyim said we killed their God. They also said that we used the blood of murdered Christian children at Passover. They would be drinking vodka—they would come into our section of the village with clubs and axes and kill and torture the Jews we hid from them. They burned houses and smashed the arms of children and threw them out the window.

TAPE: *(In Spanish and English)*
Se prendieron los niños.
They smashed babies like they were pigs.
They threw them against trees.

RAYE: They cut open the stomachs of pregnant women, and these hooligans—they abused Jewish girls right in the middle of the street.

ROSALIND: *(Standing)* I saw a Pol Pot soldier. He cut a woman's dress off with a big knife and slit her belly and took out the baby.

RAYE: Hundreds of people were yelling, "Bey Shida! Bey Shida!," which means kill the Jews.

(Pause—and freeze)

RAYE: All of the Jews had one desire—to come to the Free World, the land of promise, "di goldeneh medina".

WOMEN: *(Whispering with emotion)* Di goldeneh medina.

RAYE: So when I was still a child, my father left for America and worked for four years until he had saved up enough money to bring all of us across. He paid for my mother, my brother, and myself.
   This is what I remember about the journey: To leave Russia legally, you had to have a governor's permit.

JESSICA: *(In Yiddish)* Arloybenish!

RAYE: We couldn't afford to pay so we poor Jews had to sneak across the Russian-German border which was guarded by soldiers. You did it through these special people who led immigrants across the border illegally.

ALMA: ¡Hay viene El Coyote!

ACT ONE

GEORGE: ¡A ver como nos va con El Coyote!

RAYE: We hid in the barn and they bribed the guards to look away so at the right moment, when it was safe, they would signal to us, "Now run, run!" So we picked up our luggage and we ran until we were safe.

VOICE: *(On tape)* How did you cross the border?

PAUL: *(On tape; is from El Salvador)* I crawled across the border on my belly.

WOMAN: *(On tape, in a Cambodian accent)* I walked from Cambodia to Thailand.

RAYE: Then we were put in a house where emigrants and wanderers who had come across the border wait to take the train. That was the first time in my life I was on a train.

LENA'S VOICE: *(On tape, with a Russian/Jewish accent)* And I thought to myself in Russia, how beautiful it will be in the United States.

RAYE: Finally we got to the boat. We traveled third-class steerage, in the bowels of the ship, and as religious Jews, especially my mother, who was ultra-pious, we could not partake of the food that the ship gave us, except for herring, potatoes, and tea. It was a long journey and we were very crowded and we suffered from seasickness.... You know, they say you don't vomit when you put garlic on bread. *(Pause)* Well, it doesn't work.
   When we were able to go on deck we would exchange reminiscences, compare notes...where we came from...where we were going...hopes in the golden land of Columbus.

LENA: *(On tape)* What did I expect to find? I expected the best.

RAYE: Well, each one was dreaming his own dreams. Some were dreaming of getting wealthy. There were legends that in America you could find gold in the streets.

(Pause and freeze. All lean forward and look at "gold".)

RAYE: About four or five in the morning, we all got up. The whole ship. Everyone came out on the deck, waiting for the boat that would take us to Ellis Island.

(All at benches rise and react in broad, clichéd Italian, Jewish styles: "Mama mia! Oy vey!", etc.)

RAYE: The sun rose and what do we see? The Statue of Liberty! Well, she was beautiful in the early morning light. We could see New York...and all the tall buildings. A little boat came and took us to Ellis Island, and there were police officers, and lawyers, and judges to inspect and question us. Afterwards, they gave us some food—nice sandwiches, and the first banana we ever saw.

(Everyone at benches takes out bananas and examines them curiously, figures out whether or how to eat them.)

JOSIE: *(Holding banana)* What is this?

JESSICA: *(Slaps her hand)* Don't eat it! Don't touch it!

PAMELA: *(On microphone, old and waspy, slightly patronizing)* Ellis Island is beautifully located in upper New York Bay and enjoys an abundance of sunlight and fresh air. The view of lower New York with its amazing skyline is without parallel. The harbor has a never-ending procession of water craft, giant ocean liners, tugs, freighters, ferries, and excursion boats. These furnish variety and interest all day long for the alien if....

JESSICA: *(Interrupting, grabbing microphone. She is warm and energetic, with a heavy accent.)* The worst

ACT ONE

thing...you wouldn't guess! Every morning they came around to delouse us. You know what that means? Our clothes were taken off. No bath or anything. All they knew was how to delouse us—you should excuse me. They took our clothes and put them in the garbage. They got rid of our Jewish names, too. They couldn't say them, so they changed them. Ilya David Katz Nelonbogen—poof! Lou Katz!

RAYE: *(Takes microphone)* I saw people who didn't pass the medical examination. They were crying and begging the officer to let them stay. We were so happy that we got to stay—all of us, the whole family.

(Melancholy klezmer music begins to play.)

(The women sweep around RAYE *like strange birds.)*

(All whisper intensely.)

JESSICA: Beware! of men wearing badges who will offer to carry your baggage or take you to your destination.

JOSIE: Beware! of swindling cab drivers.

ALMA: Beware! of men who say they are lawyers or accountants.

ROSALIND: Beware! of people whose friendship is too easily made.

JESSICA: Beware! of crooked ticket agents who might buy you a ticket to the wrong destination.

PAMELA: Beware! of strangers who offer to change your money.

ROSALIND: Beware! of friendly bankers and loan sharks.

*(*WOMEN *completely encircle* RAYE.*)*

JESSICA: Beware! of those who crowd around you on your arrival and declare themselves your protectors and friends. Ask in New York how many Jews have had their hearts broken in such ways.

(Music changes to happy kletzmer music. MEN *dance upstage.)*

RAYE: When I got to New York the fun began! The first time I went out to take a walk in America with my father, I saw the streets had lights and everyone was walking up and down. My father told me they burned until morning. I saw so many men and women. I saw my first Negro. I saw a Chinaman with a braid. I saw elevated trains. I had the first ice cream of my life that night. It was wonderful!

(Music stops. ABE *speaks in a haughty 19th century style. As he speaks, the company feels their own faces.)*

ABE: To the practiced eye the physiognomy of certain groups unmistakenly proclaims inferiority of type. I have seen gatherings of the foreign born in which narrow and sloping foreheads were the rule. In every face there was something wrong—lips thick, mouth coarse, upper lip too long, cheekbones too high, chin poorly formed, the bridge of the nose hollowed, the base of the nose tilted, or else the whole face prognathous. There were so many sugar-faced, loaf-heads, moon-faces, slit-mouths, lantern jaws, and goosebill noses that one might imagine a malicious spirit had amused himself by casting human beings in a set of skewmolds by the Creator.

(The company, while taking off and discarding their old-fashioned clothes, performs the following with an unnatural heartiness:)

PAMELA: A Jew, like any other foreigner,

ROSALIND AND PAMELA: is appreciated when he lives the American social life.

JOSIE: Until then...

ACT ONE

ALMA AND JOSIE: ...he counts for nothing.

GEORGE: Join American clubs...

GEORGE AND ABE: ...read American papers.

JIM: Try to adapt yourself to the manners...

DANA: ...and customs...

ABE: ...and habits...

ALL WOMEN: ...of the American people.

DANA, JESSE, AND JIM: Become an American citizen as soon as you can!

PAMELA: And...

ALL MEN: ...join the National Guard!

PAMELA: I heard that liposuction really hurts.

JESSICA: Have you read *Men Who Love Women Who Love Men Too Much?*

PAMELA: Twice.

VOICE: *(On tape)* Do you think you will go back to El Salvador?

ROSEANNA: *(On tape)* Oh yes; it's my dream.

VOICE: *(On tape)* It is your dream?

ROSEANNA: *(On tape)* Yes, it's my dream.

(All freeze.)

JESSE: He was a victim of spirits.

ABE: What spirits?

JESSE: Spirits of this country. Last night when he died, he was watching *The Incredible Hulk.*

CUSTOMS AND COSTUMES

(A slide whistle)

(A highly stylized and vaudevillian dance and "demonstration", using precisely assembled poses, with signal props and costumes as icons; for example, a babushka, a coat, a plate of food, all of which can come from the trunk.)

(The style suggests commedia, kathelaki, bunraku. All is articulate, choreographed precisely and fast. For example, GEORGE points to JOSIE, who rushes in, wearing a babushka.)

GEORGE: *(A Latin accent)* This young Slavic woman, arriving in 1905, wears a babushka, or scarf, worn by most women from eastern and southern Europe

PAMELA: *(A snob accent)* This attractive young Indian woman is wearing a huipile, common in the Huehuetanango Department of Guatemala.

ABE: *(An Indian accent)* This group of Serbian gypsies is thought to be part of a boat load of gypsies sent back to Europe. For them, with New York so far in the background, Ellis Island was surely an island of tears.

DANA: *(A Chinese accent)* This Russian Jew, arriving in 1905, has been marked for special examination: The chalkmark on his coat shows a suspected hernia condition.

JOSIE: *(An Asian accent)* This Immigration Service officer is conducting an illegal search on this teenager at San Ysidro border station near San Diego, California.

ACT ONE 13

JESSE: *(A Jewish accent)* This is a bottle of picante hot sauce, well loved by both Asian and Hispanic immigrants.

ALMA: *(A Mexican accent)* This little dumpling, filled with meat, vegetables, or fish, is called a pierogi, or when baked, a piroshki.

RAYE: *(A red-neck accent)* This is a ravioli, the Italian cousin to pierogi, or piroshki, and to the won ton. This is a won ton. It's called the Chinese pierogi or piroshki, or Chinese ravioli. The pierogi or piroshki is called the Russian, Polish, Lithuanian won ton, or the Russian, Polish, Lithuanian ravioli.

JIM: *(A Japanese accent)* This young woman gracefully carries a water jug, often plastic, on her head.

ALMA: *(A Spanish accent)* This is nuk nam, the Vietnamese spicy fish sauce.

ABE: *(A snob accent)* This is a hot tamale.

DANA: *(An American accent)* This is lemon grass, a favorite ingredient in Thai and Vietnamese food.

JESSE: *(A Spanish accent)* These Italian men, waiting in the railroad room for the train to take them to their American destinations, have already started their box lunches.

JIM: *(Heavy Japanese accent)* This is salpicon, a favorite in Salvadorean and Nicaraguan cuisine.

JOSIE: *(Charming Asian accent)* Not gold, but this little Italian child has just found her first penny on Ellis Island.

JESSICA: *(A Jewish accent)* These are Milton and Guillermo Mendez, aged six and eight, who have been arrested as illegal aliens and are being held in El Centro Detention Center near Los Angeles, California.

ROSALIND: *(A Beverly Hills accent)* This is called a lucha, the handwoven blouse many Hmong women sell in America.

DANA: *(A Chinese accent)* This is called the tefillim which many Orthodox Jews wrap around their arms for prayer.

JESSICA: *(A Jewish accent)* This is called the cho-go-ri—the lovely blouse—and this is called a chee-ma—the lovely skirt that Korean women wear on festive occasions.

ROSALIND: *(A six o'clock news accent)* This is a Buddhist monk from Thailand. During the day, he works at Mays as a stock boy.

PAMELA: *(Same)* This young Guatemalan teenager works in a transvestite club on Santa Monica Boulevard.

(The intensity builds. A doll is thrown on the stage.)

ALMA: *(Simply)* This doll represents a Cambodian tortured by the Khmer Rouge.

(The following is a "dream" sequence. Cambodian music.)

ROSALIND: There was white everywhere...the balconies and windows were hung with sheets, towels, shirts...all white. Girls put white ribbons in their hair. Everyone was weeping and cheering. And then we saw them...the Khmer Rouge...the Pol Pot. They came from all sides of the city and marched down the main boulevard. They had been up all night fighting. People offered them flowers and bowls of rice. They were all in black with checkered scarves and Ho Chi Minh sandals. They told us that we had to leave the city; that the Americans were going to bomb. They told us that Angka would take care of us. They were very young, some just twelve or thirteen,

ACT ONE 15

and no one over eighteen. The strangest thing was that none of them smiled...no one smiled.

JIM: *(Sternly)* You are now free. There is no turning back. The revolution is here. You must choose to follow Angka or not. You must forget everything you have learned. The wheel of history is turning and you cannot stop it. If you use your hands to try to stop the wheel they will be crushed. If you use your feet you will lose them.

JOSIE: Give all your material possessions to Angka. Give your whole life to Angka. Confess your imperialist sins to Angka. Angka pardons you. Angka says nothing but it has ears everywhere. The wheel of history is turning and you cannot stop it.

ALL: Long live the courageous People's National Liberation Armed Forces of Kampuchea!

ALMA: *(In an alarmed tone)* She was a victim of spirits.

ROSALIND: What spirits?

JOSIE: Spirits of this country. Last night when she died she was watching *The Incredible Hulk.*

JESSICA: When my garden is finished, I want to have a theme party and invite Lisa and Bruce.

PAMELA: Her architect is here from France and he's absolutely adorable.

JESSICA: She knows this fabulous place for Navaho rugs in Santa Fe.

WORK

RAYE: We had two nice rooms on Allen Street. What a crowd — my father and mother, my brother, and soon after, my new baby sister. Sometimes we even had to take in a boarder to make ends meet. My

mother was so clean. She was always scrubbing and
she made her own soap. We ate good—meat once a
week. My mother fed everyone for less than a dollar.
(Pause and freeze)
   Lots of potatoes.
   On Passover, we each got an orange and some
walnuts.
   For me, the most important thing was to make some
money and to help my family. I was lucky I got a job
right away as an operator of a sewing machine in the
garment center. I made two dollars a week. Then I got
another job on Sundays.

GEORGE: *(Oily, on microphone, in the audience)* Praise
the Lord, praise the Lord. Child of God, I've got news.
I want to talk to you about your ability to earn.... It
comes from God.
   Remember that there are college graduates today
who are looking for work.
   If you recognize God's place in your life, then
you will begin to find the answer to increasing the
substance of your life. Do you really think God would
ask you to give money if he didn't give you the ability
to get the money?

JESSICA: *(As a Jewish woman, offering pieces of cake to the
audience)* So we went to work. It was child's work,
since we were all children. We had a corner in the
factory which was like a kindergarten, all children.
The work wasn't difficult. You had little scissors
because you were little children.
(To an audience member) Piece of cake, darling?
Go ahead, I made it myself.
   Somehow the boss always knew when the big
macha was coming. When the inspector came in we
were put in these big wooden cases and covered with
shmatas. He never saw any children.
(To another audience member) Go on—I can tell you're

hungry. Enjoy.
  In the busy season, we worked seven days a week. There was a sign in the freight elevator: "If you don't come in on Sunday, don't come in on Monday." Ten years later, things were different...we had organized. *(To yet another audience member)* Darling, I've got to tell you—there's a lovely man sitting all by himself in the third row. Maybe at intermission you'll say hello.

ENGLISH

(Projection: American signs, advertising, warnings, and businesses)

(Actors are hurrying to "school". On the benches, upstage, they speak in a variety of accents.)

RAYE: Next to work, the most important thing was an education. School was free in America, both for the goyim and the Jews. Most of the workers at the factory brought books to work, mainly in Yiddish, but some in Russian, German, and even English. During our lunch hour everyone would read. It was like a library. At night, people went to school.

JESSICA: Learn English! You must speak the language that all the men in America speak.

ROSALIND: Learn English! Don't spend your life on Delancey Street wasting your time in a candy store.

GEORGE: Learn English! You need to ask directions on the street.

JESSE: Learn English! You need to speak to your landlord.

ABE: Learn English! You need English to get a job and to follow directions on the job.

PAMELA: Learn English! Every year in America, hundreds of immigrants are hurt or killed because they can't read signs, when a few English words might have saved their lives.

JESSICA: One evening, I asked my evening school teacher to tell me the real difference between "I was writing" and "I have written." "What do you mean by the real difference?" he demanded. "I have told you, haven't I, that 'I was writing' is the imperfect tense while 'I have written' is the present perfect tense." "I know," I replied in my wretched English, "but what is the REAL difference between those two tenses? That's what bothers me." "Well," he said grandly, "The imperfect tense refers to what WAS, while the present perfect tense refers to what HAS BEEN."

(The company is opening their lesson books when a woman's voice, from on high, overarticulated and emotionless, paralyzes them. They respond in unison with "mudras".)

(Mudras: Lowering the head to listen carefully. Tilting the head to the side. Nodding both ways, as if to understand. Mouth agape, you don't understand.)

WOMAN'S VOICE: *(Emotionless)* What is the difference between to BURN UP and to BURN DOWN? What happens to the lights in your home when a fuse BURNS OUT? What do you do with electric lights when they BURN OUT? What does it mean to say that someone is BURNT OUT?

(Lights brighter)

(The company takes books out.)

ALL: Hello teacher. Hello teacher.

(They laboriously read from their books.)

ACT ONE   19

ALMA: *(Alone and with great effort)* Hal GOES IN for tennis while his wife GOES IN for painting and sculpture.

JOSIE: *(With great difficulty)* Kristin is INTO health food. In fact, she has become a vegetarian.

DANA: She's INTO purple this year; everything she owns is that color.

ALMA: Multiple choices!

COMPANY: Multiple choices!

(Ellis Island becomes a TV game show set. Bright lights. Game show music and canned applause. Two teams line up on either side of the stage.)

RAYE: *(As an oily, overbearing game show host, wearing a funny wig. With microphone.)* Hello everybody, and welcome to the Green Card Show, the game you have to play if you want to stay.
(He introduces PAMELA as hostess. Applause.)
Okay. Here's our two teams. From the Evans Community School we have....
(He introduces actors by name. They can improvise their responses in the way ordinary people are shy and embarrassed on live television—and in this case exacerbated by their being foreign.)
And from the Hollywood High Night School...
(He introduces actors. Wild applause.)
Now, here's how our game works. The team that answers three out of five multiple-choice questions correctly gets their green cards and stays, while the team that loses goes back, as they say, to where they belong.

(Note: Ad-libbed comments are not indicated here, but there should be plenty of them. I hope this scene will be constantly open to changes from the actors.)

RAYE: Okay? Teams, are you ready to play? Remember, every answer counts. Here's our first question!
Zan and Rich PULLED OFF one of the best jokes I've ever witnessed.
a. Yes, they always fail, don't they?
b. How did they do it?
c. Did it hurt when it came off?

(Both teams huddle in intense consultation. Hollywood rings the very loud buzzer first. JIM *gets the correct answer (b) for Hollywood High.)*

RAYE: Did you get CARRIED AWAY when you described the beauty of their garden?
a. No. I wouldn't let them lift me.
b. Yes, I left because I hated it.
c. Yes, I even started to cry.

*(*ABE *gets the correct answer, (c). Wild applause.)*

RAYE: Okay, teams, we're tied. Let's see which team is going to break the tie. Listen carefully for question number three: What is the most personal use of the expression "to lose one's cool"?
a. Despite the disturbing heckler in the audience, Ms. Skutnick never loses her cool.
b. John needed to put ice cubes in his coffee.
c. Pepe always loses his cool when someone insults his mother.

*(*JESSICA *gets the correct answer, (c).)*

RAYE: Good answer. This means Evans Community School is leading by one point. One more correct answer and they win. Here's our fourth multiple-choice problem:
I think I'll TAKE PITY on those people who are begging for money.
a. I feel sorry for them, too.

ACT ONE

b. I can't stand them either.
c. I would rather subscribe to another magazine.

(DANA, *in his excitement, answers in Chinese. Everyone admonishes him—"English, English!" Canned audience boos. He answers in English and Hollywood High scores a point. The excitement mounts.*)

RAYE: This is very exciting, folks. We've got another tie. Here's the big tie breaker, the last question of the game. If neither team answers correctly, they both get sent back to where they belong.

(*The entire Evans team kneels down to pray. The atmosphere is absolutely frantic and charged.*)

RAYE: The question is: What is the most contemporary use of the expression to TURN ONE ON or to TURN ONE OFF?
a. Pretty women certainly TURN Charlie ON?
b. Some of the great Renaissance painters TURN me ON but some of the modern ones TURN me OFF.
c. Minimalist post-modern performance art of the 1980s is a real TURN OFF for me.

(GEORGE *of the Evans team tries and fails with (b).* ALMA *answers correctly with (c). The Hollywood High team is jubilant. Lights fade.*)

RAYE: That's right.... Here's our winner!

(*All freeze.* JOSIE *wheels a blackboard out. She is isolated in light as, with painstaking deliberation and care, she writes her name: Eang Him Huoy. It is the first time she has written her name in English script. She finishes, turns, and proudly smiles to no one.*)

(*The lights fade very slowly.*)

NATIVES

(All move through the space as if searching for something, perhaps a lost thought.)

JIM: The simple truth is that the dilation of people and institutions in this country has gone too far.

ABE: With the Mexicans already here, with the as-yet unassimilated immigrants from certain European countries, and finally with the vast and growing Negro population, we already have an almost superhuman task to bring about the requisite national unity.

JIM: In the matter of Chinese and Japanese coolie immigration I stand for exclusion.

ABE: During the entire settlement in California, they have never learned the sanctity of an oath, never desired to become citizens, never discovered the difference between right and wrong, never ceased the worship of their idol gods. They remain the same stolid Asiatics that have floated on the rivers and slaved in the fields of Asia for thirty centuries.

Either the Anglo-Saxon race will possess the Pacific slope or the Mongolians will possess it.

ROSALIND: Confucius say....

(She stops, frozen in a suspended and anguished pose.)

JESSE: He was a victim of spirits.

JIM: What spirits?

JESSE: Spirits of this country. Last night when he died he was watching *The Incredible Hulk*.

(Music. High thin giggles as group of boat people forms upstage)

ACT ONE 23

ROSALIND: *(In a falsely delicate "Asian" accent)* Long experience with foreign domination has taught the people of Indochina a wariness of strangers.

PAMELA: *(Harsh and crudely direct)* DID YOU WORK FOR THE AMERICAN GOVERNMENT IN SAIGON? HOW DID YOU ESCAPE SAIGON? IS IT TRUE THAT THERE WERE MANY CASES OF RAPE, ROBBERY, AND MURDER BY THAI PIRATES ON THE HIGH SEAS?

JOSIE: *(To the audience, in the same "Asian" style)* The people of Vietnam possess an inwardness and a well-developed ability to keep their true feelings hidden.

ROSALIND: Vietnamese consider it impolite to point.

JOSIE: American straightforwardness is considered impolite, if not brutal.

PAMELA: ARE YOU HAPPY HERE? DO YOU THINK AMERICANS APPRECIATE ASIAN CULTURE?

BOAT PEOPLE: *(Drawing a blank)* Huh?

JOSIE: The essence is not whether the question is true or false but what is the intention of the speaker. Does it indicate a wish to change the subject?

ROSALIND: Does it facilitate interpersonal harmony?

PAMELA: ARE YOU AFRAID THAT YOUR CHILDREN WILL FORGET YOUR LANGUAGE AND CULTURE?

JOSIE: *(Silence)* Hence one must learn the heart of the subject.

DANA: *(Breaking away from the group, as* MARSHALL KY. *He is wearing a trim leather jacket, aviator glasses, a purple silk scarf, and is smoking a French cigarette.)* Look, once and for all, I want to set the record straight. I never was involved in the so-called Vietnamese Mafia. Did you see Mike Wallace? He said there was no proof.

I came here with forty-thousand dollars and I had thirteen relatives waiting to be supported. I was a refugee. Like all the others, I slept in a tent in Camp Pendleton. Of course, I was better known. In fact, for a while I suppose you could say I, Marshall Nguyen Cao Ky, was the most famous refugee in America. That's why I went on the lecture circuit. I needed the money, and my agent said I'd only be good for a year. I went to places like Iowa City, staying in Holiday Inns with my wife Mai, and was heckled by acne-faced kids. Mai started ordering gin and tonic here. You heard about Vietnamization. I call that Americanization. *(He laughs.)* Everyone was upset because I bought a silver-grey Cadillac. Look, I bought it on credit.... Credit, what an American trap.

I left a fantastic wardrobe, designer jumpsuits from Paris, and a beautiful record collection and a dozen cases of Tabasco sauce. Once I got here, I made it my business to study all the American businesses, things like fast food-franchises—McDonald's, Gino's...things like that. And I came to the conclusion that the liquor store is the safest small American business. OK. It didn't work out. I went bankrupt. Then Mai lost $10,000—

JOSIE: $20,000.

DANA: —$20,000 at Caesar's Palace in a baccarat game. And then her boutique failed. Now, I'm going to start a chain of Vietnamese fast-food restaurants. Americans are crazy about ethnic food, right?

(The company breaks into aggressive high style.)

JOSIE: *(A Vietnamese accent)* Hey! What's a favorite Vietnamese cookbook?

ACT ONE 25

(Company, clichéd "Vietnamese" laugh and gesture)

JESSICA: *(A Jewish accent)* What do Polish lesbians do on a date?

(Company, clichéd "Jewish" laugh and gesture)

ABE: *(An Italian accent)* What's an Italian innuendo?

(Company, clichéd "Italian" laugh and gesture)

JIM: *(A Japanese accent)* What do Japanese do during erection?

(Company, clichéd "Japanese" laugh and gesture)

ALMA: *(A Mexican accent)* How does a Mexican cross the border?

(Ear-piercing whistle. Group turns together.)

IMMIGRATION

(Moving lights from above and side: Helicopter searchlights)

(A slow-motion dance of backs and shoulders to Brian Eno and David Byrnes' "The Carrier." The dance represents a stylized "crossing the border".)

PAMELA: *(Blows whistle)* You do not have to appear in person and wait in long lines at the Immigration Service.

(Company faces audience.)

RAYE: Fast and reliable information and assistance in all immigration matters.

(The following is performed at break-neck speed, barely intelligible.)

PAMELA: At Immigration Service we will....

JOSIE: Explain to you in detail all your immigration questions. Provide necessary forms....

JESSE: Twenty-five dollars.

ALMA: Extension of B1, B2, visa. Provide necessary forms.

PAMELA: Twenty dollars.

RAYE: Prepare and submit your applications to the Immigration and provide all necessary forms.

ROSALIND: Twenty dollars.

JIM: Obtain a receipt from the Immigration Service and provide the necessary forms.

GEORGE: Ten dollars.

JESSE: Explain and fill out family amnesty applications.

RAYE: $1,000.

JESSICA: We also handle all other immigration matters.

ABE: Lost green card.

PAMELA: Green card for refugees.

JOSIE: Re-entry permit.

RAYE: Change of status to permanent resident of U.S.A.

ALMA: Investor visa.

DANA: Working visa.

JESSICA: Labor certification.

ROSALIND: U.S. citizenship.

JESSE: Political asylum.

GEORGE: Petition for permanent resident.

JIM: Suspension of deportation.

ALL: Take a number!

TAPE: *(English class at the Indo-Chinese refugee center. The sentence which is being laboriously practiced in a variety of Asian accents is:)* I am talking to the Immigration Office.

(During the tape, all assume positions for a frozen tableau: JESSICA as a Jewish Woman; RAYE as an Ellis Island Immigration Officer; JESSE as an Illegal Alien; JIM as a California Immigration Officer; all face each other.)

(The others form a line. It is tense, weary, anxious. The entire tableau speaks of guarded expectancy. It is held for a long time. The tension builds and is abruptly broken by the Immigration Officer handing the Jewish Woman a Bible for her to read.)

(The others face the audience and "watch a movie", whispering comments, laughing.)

RAYE: Read from this Bible.

JESSICA: *(Reading Bible in broken English)* He hath also prepared for him the instruments of death.

JIM: *(To the Hispanic Man, who is contorted with fear)* ¿Donde vives? Where do you live?

JESSE: *(In broken English)* I live in Los Angeles.

JIM: What is your address? Come on, man, ¿Qué es tu domicilio? ¿Cómo se llamo, yo? ¿Cómo se llamo, yo?

JESSICA: *(Reading)* Behold, he travaileth with inequity....

JIM	RAYE:
What is your address?	Are you married?
Where do you go to	What is your
high school?	occupation?
Are you married?	Where were you born?
What is your birth date?	What is the date of your
What is your birth place?	birth?
Where did you get	Where

these papers?
Have you ever been
arrested?
How many times have
you been arrested?
Are you a citizen of
El Salvador?
How many times have you
come to the United States?
How many times
have you been caught
by Immigration officials?
Where did you cross?
When and at what time?
How many persons crossed
with you?
Where are you
going?
did
you last
reside?
Where is your ship's
manifest tag?
Where are you
going?
By whom was your
passage paid?
Is that person
in the United States
now?
If so, for how long?
How do you intend
to support yourself in
the United States?
Are you an anarchist?
Are you a polygamist?

What kind of job are you looking for? Who were you going to meet in Los Angeles? What is your address? What is your home telephone number?
(Trick question. Intensity builds.)
COME ON, MAN! WHAT IS YOUR HOME TELEPHONE NUMBER?

(JESSE *tries out various numbers in a confusion of Spanish and English.*)

JESSICA: ...and is fallen into the ditch he made.

PAMELA: *(On microphone to the audience; bright and quick)* The committee recommends that the following be excluded: Idiots, imbeciles, feeble-minded persons and mental defectives, insane persons, persons of constitutional psychopathic inferiority, persons with chronic alcoholism, persons certified as mentally defective, persons afflicted with tuberculosis in any form, persons afflicted with a loathsome or dangerous contagious disease. The list now includes bigamists,

ACT ONE

homosexuals, and drug addicts.

(PAMELA *puts down mike, starts upstage, stops, turns back to audience.*)

Oh, yeah, and in 1917, revolutionaries were added.

JIM: En este lugar, usted no tiene derechas.
In this place, you have no rights.

ALMA: *(In a stage whisper, as if talking across a row of people at a movie theater:)* Psst! Hey! Era un victimo de los espiritos.

ABE: ¿Qué espiritos?

(Group still whispering and obviously irritating others.)

ALMA: Espiritos de este pais. Anoche cuando murió estuviera viendo *El Incredible Hulk*.

(Lights start to fade.)

(Long light fade)

(Neon arrow flies in.)

PAMELA: I loved the prawn tamale with cilantro-oregano butter.

JESSICA: Equally impressive is the zuni pizza with duck sausage, roasted garlic, and poblano chiles.

PAMELA: The quesadilla with shitake mushrooms, Sonoma goat cheese, and pine nuts was subtle yet assertive.

JESSICA: Yes.

CALIFORNIA

(Opening chords of The Mamas and the Papas' "California Dreamin'." The set becomes California—palm trees, neon, blue skies. Company, wearing Hawaiian shirts, dances, shouting the following

words, which are repeated twice. The words can be changed.)

RAYE: Malibu.

JIM: Hollywood.

JESSICA: Salad bar.

JESSE: Ready Teller.

ABE: Jacuzzi.

ROSALIND: Plastic surgery

JOSIE: New Age.

DANA: Drive-thru.

GEORGE: Muscle Beach.

ALMA: Valet parking.

PAMELA: 1-hour dry cleaning.

RAYE: Happy hour.

JIM: Suntan.

JESSICA: Roller skating.

JESSE: Carphone.

ABE: Soul food.

ROSALIND: Health food.

JOSIE: Fast food.

DANA: Freeway.

(The actors stride around the stage proudly saying:)

JIM: My name is Brian.

JOSIE: My name is Tracy.

ABE: My name is Chuck.

ROSALIND: My name is Kathy.

JESSE: My name is Darren.

ACT ONE

PAMELA: My name is Terri.

DANA: My name is Eric.

JESSICA: My name is Tammy.

RAYE: My name is Dustin.

ALMA: My name is Debbie.

GEORGE: My name is Kevin.

(This is repeated over and over as music fades.)

ABE: *(As a Latin nerd)* California es un pais turisticamente todo el tiempo. Ya que sus centros diversion como los son Disneylandia, Montaña Magica, Sea World, Museo de Cera de Hollywood, el Mark Taper Forum y playas, atraen a turistas del interior del pais, asi como de otros lugares del mundo, y no solo en tiempo de los L. A. Lakers.

ALL: Go Lakers!

ABE: Si no verano, otoño, primavera, e invierno.

GEORGE: I finally got to Tijuana, then I crossed there through a coyote. We walked all night to Escondido. From there we went to Los Angeles. They took us in a false back of a car to a place in L. A. where there were just people from Central America and Mexico. I thought when I got here, I would be living with Americans.

(Lights dim.)

ALMA: *(Isolated in light, clutching a shopping bag)* I always take the bus to work and I'm really afraid. People get picked up at the bus stop. I've only been here two years. I couldn't prove the amnestia.
    One of my ladies, she likes me so much, she always drives me home. I'm glad I have this work, it's okay. It's not so bad, except for the gringo children. They're really messy. The lady, I think she's ashamed.

I always start with the kitchen, the refrigerator first. That's the biggest job. They tell me to throw out food or they give me food to take home. They have Chinese food, and different food left over in cartons. The freezer is so big, it's filled with steaks and coffee from all over the world, and they even have special meat for their dogs and cats.

I clean the tops of everything with Fantastik. I mop the kitchen floor with Mr. Clean. You have to get down on your hands and knees to clean the corners.

Next I do the bathroom. They always have more than one bathroom. Sometimes even they have three. I use Windex on the glass shelves. They keep a lot of things in their bathrooms. They have special soaps, other things. I'm not sure what they are...creams and oils for your face and body. They have scales for weighing themselves. After the bathroom, I do the bedrooms or whatever other rooms they have. They have rugs that cover the whole house...every room. I vacuum these rugs. I never saw a vacuum cleaner before I came here. What a machine! They have attachments. These attachments do all kinds of special cleaning.

Then I make all the beds with two sheets that match. I put special polish on the furniture. One of my ladies taught me how to do it. Some of the people, they have special paintings and statues and things like bicycles that they exercise on, but they don't go nowhere. Afterwards I go home and take care of my daughter, Angelica. They don't let me bring her to work. My house...well, it's not so clean. You know, after cleaning other people's houses all day, I don't feel like cleaning my own house.

I never go out because I don't know how to get around here and I'm tired at night. There are some things I'd like to see in L. A., but mostly I watch T.V. *(She takes* TV Guide *out of her bag and reads in a*

ACT ONE 33

fractured accent. She can barely read it.)
   Tonight on *LA Law*, Van Owen (Susan Dey), after the untimely death of a client, escapes to Maui to contemplate life's vicissitudes and finds romance!

(Bright lights. The company is all over the set. The effect is of rapidly switching T.V. channels. Lines overlay. Performers "leap out", briefly take bows, then recede. All the information in this "T.V. show" can be updated so that it is current.)

GEORGE: This is Geraldo Rivera. Today, housewives with X-rated pants busts.

RAYE: Praise the Lord. Come here, darling, don't be afraid. You know I'm not going to hurt you.

ALMA AND ABE: *(Wesson Oil commercial)* Todo es mas rico con Wesson Oil, Wesson Oil.
Todo es mas rico con Wesson Oil, Wesson Oil!

JESSE: ¿Esté solo? ¿Buscé pareja? ¿Cansado de que nadie la invita a cenar y a bailar? Mandenos una carta describiendo su persona y diendonos que tipo de persona la gustaria conocer.

PAMELA: *(Overlapping)* Praise the Lord. John in a motel room in Oklahoma on the verge of suicide found Jesus.

DANA: And it's going to be a beautiful weekend. Hot and sunny and very clean air. So get ready, Southlanders.

(JOSIE, GEORGE, and JESSICA, exercising on the floor.)

GEORGE: Okay, now lie on the floor and knee to chest, knee to chest.

JESSICA: Tighten that buttock and the front of the thigh. Can you feel it? Inhale. Exhale. Inhale. Exhale.

(Spanish soap opera)

ABE: ¡Tengo una confesión!

ALMA: Dime, Armando.

ABE: Marcela, he perdido todo nuestro dinero.

ALMA: ¡Qué escéndalo! Dame el cigarillo.

PAMELA: Went to the opening night party at Pink, the hottest new spot in Santa Monica.

JOSIE: *(While exercising)* The latest beating is not the first incidence of violence by young blacks towards Asians in Los Angeles.

GEORGE: This is Geraldo Rivera. Tomorrow: Right-wing Central American death squads in Los Angeles?

JIM: I think we can say that Satanic worship is about an individualistic approach to the world.

PAMELA: One-half of the groups use human blood.

ROSALIND: *(Arms out, bouncing from side to side)* You don't have to jump around to get that heart up. Let's swing with it and kind of dance and dance and dance....

GEORGE: This is Geraldo Rivera. When we come back we're going to talk about something that makes no American proud: Mass murder.

(Spanish soap opera)

ALMA: Armando, yo tambien tengo una confesión.

ABE: Acaso algo te angustia.

ALMA: Sí. Tengo amantel.

ABE: ¡Que horror! Dame el cigarillo!

DANA: *(As a clichéd "Chinaman")* Kill me, I must preserve my honor.

ROSALIND: *(Same cliché)* Stay out of Chinatown.

ACT ONE

RAYE: I'm a jogger. You mentioned sacrificing chickens. In my jogging, I see a lot of dead chickens. How does this affect me as a Christian?

JESSICA: Is your life slipping out of control? We can help.

GEORGE: Dianetica!

JOSIE: A report on the so-called refugee dream-death syndrome.

JIM: One thousand police officers swept through gang-infested neighborhoods and rounded up twenty gang members.

PAMELA: Then it's off to Mr. Chow's in Beverly Hills for a champagne-saturated feast hosted by New York's Bianca Jagger.

JESSE: No, Bob, I was just a victim of bondage until I found Jesus.

ABE: ¡Me voy!

ALMA: ¿A dónde? *(As* ABE *begins)* Qué?

ABE: Arby's. No. Friendly's. No, Benny's. No, Denny's.

JESSE: *(Interrupting. As a rock 'n roll, reggae, rap solo. The company becomes ecstatic, as* JESSE's *performance gains intensity.)*
Arby's
Friendly's
Benny's
Denny's
Hardee's
Shakey's
Blimpies
Wimpy's
Wienerschnitzel
Wally's World of Waffles

Arthur Treacher's
Howard Johnson's
Famous Amos
Ponderosa
Pizzarama
Burgerama
Fooderama
Fisherama
Porkarama
Burger Chef
Burger Town
Burger Time
Burger City
Burger World
Burger Heaven
Burger Palace
Burger Haven
Burger 'n Bun
Bun 'n Run
Tons of Buns
House of Buns
House of Toast
House of Pancakes
Jack in the Box
Roy Roger's
Marv's
Bill's
Bob's
Joe's Bo's
Brian's Spanish Anna's
Ralph's Cabana
Red Lobster
Brown Derby
Yellow Fingers
Purple Onion
Orange Julius
White Castle

ACT ONE

White Tower
Tuesday's
Wednesday's
Thursday's
Friday's
Pizza Hut
Pizza Palace
Pizza Time
Time for Tacos
Taco Bell
Bell Taco
Del Taco
El Taco
Taco Tico
Tico's Tacos
Bagel Nosh
Adam's Rib
Little Bit O' Heaven
Little Bit O' Chicken
McCay's
McAnn's
McDonald's

ROSALIND: I love that!

(Everyone but ALMA *faints.)*

JESSICA: Is your life slipping out of control? We can help.

ALMA: La ciencia moderna de la salud mental.

GEORGE: *(On microphone; at breakneck speed, as an Hispanic radio commerical)* ¡Dianetica! ¿Busca resolver sus problemas en la vida? Descubre en Dianetica porque sus problemas no lo dejan progresar. En Dianetica encontrará technicas de como relajarse. Dianetica! Sea una persona liberada, triufadora, y a poder de si misma. Dianetica! Por L. Ron Hubbard. A solo quatro dolares.

(The following is performed in a disquietingly earnest style, with the performers moving into the house and quietly and seriously addressing their questions in a "personal" manner to members of the audience.)

RAYE: Do you live the kind of existence where you have only a few expressions of enthusiasm?

ABE: Do you have any persistent mannerisms, like pulling your hair, nose, ears, and such?

JESSICA: When recounting some humorous event, are you able to skillfully imitate the mannerisms or dialect of the original event?

ROSALIND: If you saw something in a shop which was clearly marked lower than its actual price, would you try to buy it at that price?

JIM: Is it sometimes hard for you to totally enter the spirit of things?

JESSICA: Do you sometimes get quite thrilled?

DANA: Do children unnerve you?

GEORGE: Do you sleep soundly?

ALMA: Do you grin too much?

JOSIE: Do you eat too fast?

RAYE: When you're surprised, do some of your muscles have jerking motions?

ABE: Does emotional music have a powerful effect on you?

ROSALIND: Do you sometimes ask yourself if anyone cares about you?

RAYE: Would it take a deliberate effort for you to consider the subject of suicide?

GEORGE: Do you bite your nails or chew pencils?

ACT ONE

PAMELA: If you were invading a foreign country, would you feel sympathy for conscientious objectors in that country?

DANA: Do your muscles occasionally twitch when there is no real reason for it?

JOSIE: Do you hum or whistle just for the heck of it?

JIM: Does your facial expression vary or does it remain calm?

PAMELA: When you pass a beautiful child, do you avoid looking or smiling?

ALMA: Are you a barrel of laughs at a social gathering?

JESSICA: Do you think you have many warm friends?

RAYE: After seing a tragic movie or play, do you quickly return to normal?

ABE: Does life sometimes seem sort of hazy and unreal to you?

JESSE: *(Slowly walking back onto the stage)* Well, it didn't work out. One day...it was last May when I had only been here nine months, and I was waiting in the usual place for a job pick-up, a police car came by. They questioned us and then they arrested us, me and another guy from El Salvador.

I think it was the woman that we worked for the day before who turned us in. They took us downtown and said they were going to look into our status. They took us to the Department of Immigration and started to question us.

I was charged with resisting arrest and then they tried to get me to talk by beating me on the back with sticks in front of other Salvadoreans who had been arrested. After being in jail in Pasadena for two months, they took me to jail in San Diego. It was hard there. They ask you a question in English and if you don't answer in English, they hit you.

I spent the rest of my time in El Centro. It's one big piece of dirt with barbed wire around it. They call it a detention center, but it's really a jail. The total time I spent in jail was five months and ten days. The majority of the people in El Centro are Salvadoreans waiting to be deported. Some of them have been there for over a year.

Once I got sent to the hole for talking back to a guard. It's a room where you can't stand up; there is no bed, no light, no window; completely enclosed. You can't hear...only a hole. I didn't know if it was night or day. They feed you through that hole. It was pretty shitty being there, not knowing what was going on with my friends.

The people in El Centro are depressed. It's not knowing what will happen. That's terrible. It's so bad that some say "I'll just go back. So what if I get killed."

In El Centro it's 110 degrees outside. There's nothing to do. If you want to go to the library, you must go with a guard. There a few books there, like the Bible. You have to wait for hours to make a call. Even if you find a lawyer to help you, you can't tell him to call back because they took the number off the phone. El Centro...it's near L.A.

(Music: Jimmy Cliff "The American Dream". JESSE walks off stage. Golden door lights up.)

END ACT ONE

ACT TWO

PROLOGUE

(As house lights go down there are slides of "god" images [carvings, sculptures, photos] on the scrim, to Terry Allen's "My Country 'tis of Thee". During the music, various cast members carry out and place three high Vietnamese water puppets on the edge of the stage. The puppets remain on stage for the entire second act, both as witnesses and as participants. GEORGE *enters in front of the scrim and addresses the audience.)*

GEORGE: *(In a comically exaggerated Hispanic accent)* The Americans did something about twenty years ago. They sent crop dusters over the swamps to kill the mosquitoes because we had malaria. After that, they wanted to clean up the country because there was so much dysentery. This is because people have no place to relieve themselves. So they sent several thousand latrines called portable toilets.

They were blue plastic, with doors and ventilation, and we were explained the use of chemicals to get rid of waste.
(Suddenly drops accent, very direct and serious)
We lived in houses made of cardboard, washing machine boxes cut apart, and scrap wood. *(Big pause)* We thought, how can we live in a cardboard box and shit in a plastic house?
(Resumes accent with even more exaggeration)
So this is what we did. We took apart the latrines

and used the materials to make better homes. Even now out in the countryside, you will find the blue toilet seats scattered around.

(JESSICA *and* PAMELA *rushing by*)

PAMELA: I stopped using Laslo when someone told me that all of a sudden when you're fifty, your face just suddenly cracks and you really look old.

JESSICA: You know they absolutely refused to park Tim Leary's old Mercedes.

PAMELA: I heard that it's your body's inability to absorb potassium. I think you're supposed to eat bananas or broccoli. I'm not sure which.

JESSICA: I can't believe her Lhasa Apso took a dump on my Navaho rug.

DANA: *(As* MARSHALL KY. *This speech is accompanied by slides of the fall of Saigon, including the famous helicopter on the roof of the American embassy.)* I went to a pot luck dinner in Iowa. It was so cold. Thirty Vietnamese families were there. You know what they said? They said they had to have hope that they were going to return to Vietnam. They said that if they had no hope, they were going to kill themselves. What could I say? I said, have hope.

I left on April 29, 1975, just hours before Saigon fell. I wanted to stay and fight. Look, I may not be a great politician, but everyone knows I was a great soldier. My plan was to make Saigon a Stalingrad, evacuate the women, children, and old people, blow up all the bridges, isolate Saigon, and fight to the death. But I couldn't do it alone. I'm not a one-man army. So I flew my helicopter to Midway aircraft carrier—you know it was the same helicopter that Westmoreland had traded me for a soccer field. Then I threw the pearl-handled revolver that John Wayne gave me after it. When I got to the States, John Wayne never

ACT TWO   43

called, and in Washington, Mai and I were never
invited to parties. Mai said that at least the French
don't pretend to like you. Americans are always
saying that they'll call you and they never do.

*(Terry Allen's "Nobody's Going Home". The company
dances upstage of scrim, while slides play of Asians and
Latins down town.)*

("Asian" music. JOSIE *is very "Oriental". She performs
with company in a corny* King and I *style.)*

JOSIE: The people of Vietnam trace their origins to the
marriage of Lac Long Quan, the Dragon Lord of Lac
from the Land of the Red Demons, and Au Co, the
daughter of a Chinese emperor. When Au Co gave
birth to a sack of eggs from which one hundred sons
were hatched, Lac Long Quan became unhappy with
his wife. They each parted. The father took his fifty
sons south to the Kingdom of Waters and the mother
took hers north to a place near present-day Hanoi.
In 208 BC....

DANA: *(As a Chinese movie warlord)* Trieu Da, a
Chinese warlord, marched south and conquered the
people of the Red River Delta. He named the country
Nam Viet.

JOSIE: The Vietnamese accepted much of the Chinese
way of life, but they refused to accept Chinese rule.
In 40 AD the Trung sisters, who were Vietnamese
patriots, raised an army to try to beat the Chinese.
The Chinese fought back and the Trung sisters
committed suicide by drowning themselves in the
river. After that, the Vietnamese became masters at
guerrilla warfare. By 1787, Vietnam was back under
one Vietnamese ruler.

(The company applauds.)

JESSICA: I loved that.

JOSIE: Then the French came....
Then the Americans came....
Now in Vietnam...

(Music: Country and western)

(Performers move the Vietnamese water puppets away from the edge of stage.)

PAMELA: I have this fascinating new teacher. He combines massage with mantra.

JESSE: I'm looking into my Jewishness. I know it's out but I think I need it now.

DANA: *(As* MARSHALL KY*)* Everyone was joining the Buddhists...trying to get me to resign. It was a mess. First, the monks, then the students, who you know were just stooges for the Vietcong, then the workers, and finally an entire division of the army. Even the police were sympathizers. It was a civil war within a civil war, and the Americans were calling us ingrates. The monks they weren't reasonable, they would rile themselves up. Everytime they didn't get their way they would sit down and burn themselves to death, and Madame Nhu made everything worse by calling it a barbecue.
    I realized that the time had come for a showdown with the Buddhists, especially Trich Tri Quang. You remember that toothy monk who managed to attract all the media attention? I think he counted on me not going against him because I myself was a Buddhist. He was on a hunger strike and I had him arrested. You know, later when the communists came, they also put him in prison. He refused to fly their flag! Quang was a ruthless political opportunist.
Americans think Buddhists are very pure...that's one of the pitfalls of Western thinking.

ACT TWO 45

JIM: Buddhism is the enemy of Angkar, it is imperialist ideology. It brings nothing but confusion and distraction to people's minds.

RELIGION

(An enormous gold Buddha comes onstage with a neon halo. The stage becomes some kind of representation of Angkor Wat—perhaps a painted drop—with sound and projection of jungle. The jungle sounds continue more or less intensely through the rest of Act Two.)

JOSIE: *(Perhaps reading)* According to Buddhism, life is a vast sea of suffering. In effect, the vicious circle of existence is renewal in the course of endless reincarnations. The cause of suffering is desire; desire for happiness, riches, or power. The essence of Buddhist teaching is contained in the concept of Karma, the present existence is conditioned by earlier existences and will condition those that follow. Thus the virtuous person should strive constantly to improve by doing good deeds and by renouncing sensual pleasures in order to become conscious of Buddha, who is present in every living being. Consequently, desire must be first overcome and a pure heart is necessary to break the chains binding one to an early existence in order to reach the state of bliss called Nirvana.

(During the above ALMA slowly says the Stations of the Cross.)

(Vietnamese temple chanting)

COLONIALISM

(During the tape [below], PAMELA slowly enters through dappled light, wearing an elegant white linen dress, eating fruit, and fanning herself. Turquoise china silk curtains trip in, with jungle projected on them.)

A WOMAN'S VOICE: *(On tape)* The woods near the city of Dvaravati and the flowering gardens echoed to the song of the birds and the humming of bees. Over its pools strewn with lotus flowers resounded the piercing cry of the flamingoes and cranes.

Its nine hundred-thousand crystal palaces sparkled with huge emeralds and furniture of gold and silver.

It was lit with the blaze of innumerable lamps of precious stones, and on its graceful roofs, O King! The peacocks danced and screamed. The crossroads, the markets, the houses, the assembly halls, and the dwellings of the gods all gave to its beauty. The streets were watered and the fluttering flags and banners gave protection from the heat.

(People enter with offerings and do prostrations to the Buddha during PAMELA's speech.)

PAMELA: It was this absolutely marvelous city...ochre. There was something about the tropical light you know...the utter steaminess of the place...the green in that light...the green of those trees on the boulevards... all kinds of trees, wild guava, flame trees, with their red and yellow blossoms...and the flowers! Hibiscus, jasmine, frangipane.

The French did it, you know. They had a flawless instinct for the boulevard. They were so good with Asia. The food was sensational. You could get anything, from café filtre at the Hotel Royal, to very fine opium after a lovely dinner at the Cafe de Paris.

ACT TWO

As for Saigon, it is sexy in a primitive sort of way, but it is certainly not the Paris of the East. Actually it's more like Nîmes. The women were always quite sweet in their little black pajamas. The French never took them as mistresses. They're too serious.
 Phnom Penh...even the name.... Everyone sitting in the shade of the boulevard...those perfect groups of little monks in their perfect orange robes with their perfect little umbrellas.
 And of course the people are quite tall you know, and they don't yammer and squawk like the Thai or Chinese...the way the women drape their sampots...it's so serene, so Buddhist.
 I loved leaving the city...gliding by the teak forests and rice paddies...teak for a thousand years.... You had to leave early in the morning. The humidity was absolutely staggering. We used to stop at the markets on the way to Angkor Wat...stunning arrangements of mangoes, coconuts, oranges, pineapples, lotus buds, water lilies. There were these little villages with adorable thatched houses around sweet Buddhist pagodas.
 I can't remember exactly when it was that all those little Sorbonne-educated revolutionaries came back to the country. They had these awful drab little brown suits. Although I must say I adore what they did with the Pol Pot outfits, that combination of red and white-checkered scarves and the black shorts on that lovely brown skin, with the Ho Chi Minh sandals...it's heavenly. You know about the Ho Chi Minh sandals? They would just take pieces of tire rubber and then they would just lash them to their little feet with strips of inner tubing. You know, Jackie Kennedy got the idea for those off-the-shoulder gowns from the monks at Angkor Wat. Sihanouk invited her. Sihanouk...he was impossible...so irritating...that voice...and those endless speeches on Radio Phnom Penh. And that

wife, Monique. I never thought she was that pretty.
She was all right.
He could be quite thoughtful, though. You know,
before the dedication of the Friendship Highway,
which we built, he actually ordered his Minister of
Public Works to drive 125 miles to Sihanoukville and
flush all of the toilets in the rest house, just to make
sure they were in working order. Of course, when we
all got there, three of them weren't working.
You know, the French detested him. I wonder
where he is now? Someone said Paris, or is it Peking?

CULTURE

(Music: Andean or Cambodian)

GEORGE: Sometimes in the countryside you will come
upon a tree that has been decorated with strips of
paper, rags, and garbage. This is because the tree
failed to bear fruit in its good year. The people
tie things to the tree to make it feel ashamed, to
embarrass it in front of other trees, so that the next
year fruit will come. One day in the campo, in an area
where there had been some killings, there was a tree
with skin and hair hanging from its branches. It
looked like rags and garbage. The soldiers who had
done this were from the campo. They knew what it
means to hang things on a tree.

(A dance with the puppets)

ALMA: *(In Spanish)* Antes que llegaron los
conquistadores españoles, la jente creo que el hombre
era de mais, en ves de barro, en que diós dió el viento.
(Before the Spanish Conquest, the people believed
that man was made from corn, rather than a piece of
clay breathed upon by God.)

ACT TWO 49

JESSICA: Pregnant women tell their babies the names of all they see in the woods, plants, flowers, animals, birds.

DANA: *(In English and Cambodian)* For thousands of years, the Khmer people have lived through a cycle of monsoons and drought, of the earth flooded and then parched.

ROSALIND: *(In Cambodian)* Bail dail kyeum tang a kneer dal knong brey madai keim ban kchap ongoa neng slock chev dck tvai neak da dam pluv. (When we passed through the woods, my mother wrapped a few grains of rice in a leaf and placed it on the ground as gift to the local spirits.)

ABE: *(In Spanish)* Before planting we ask the earth for permission to make a wound in it, because for us the earth is sacred.

JESSE: When a baby is born, he has a nahual, an animal spirit.

GEORGE: *(In English and Spanish)* Pito is a wooden flute, but it is also a vegetable that can be mixed with meat to make you sleep.

JOSIE: *(In Vietnamese)* Chung toi chon cat to tien o dong ruong. Va linh hon ho trong chung chung to. (We bury our ancestors in rice fields and their spirits watch over us.)

ROSALIND: Who in your family has been "disappeared"?

JESSE: My father, Rigoberto Morales.
My brother, Máynor Morales.
My brother, Otto Raúl Morales.
My brother, Armando Roberto Morales.
My uncle, Moisés Morales.
My uncle, Salomón Morales.
My aunt, Lilián Aida Morales.

My aunt, Elizabeth Morales.
My aunt, Sipriana Ramírez de Morales.
My cousin, Damaris Marleni Morales.
My cousin, Matia Victoria Morales.
My cousin, Héctor Manolo Morales.
My cousin, Noé Salomón Morales.
My cousin, Byron Moisés Morales.
My cousin, Abygail Morales.
My cousin, Claudia Roxana Morales.

JESSICA: I met this really attractive Panamanian sculptor last night. He's making a bust of Noriega.

PAMELA: Passive exercise works, but it only lasts for a month.

JESSICA: Do you realize that if you get silicone implants, your breasts will last forever?

PAMELA: Isn't that what they did to Eva Peron?

C.I.A.

(RAYE *and* JIM *enter with dark glasses, white shirts, and a slide projector à la 1960. They present a slide show of Cambodian people. The company and puppets watch.*)

RAYE: *(Tapping mike)* Are we live here? Can you lower that screen please? They call themselves the Khmer — that's also the name of their language.
  For the most part they are a pretty simple people, passive and docile, with limited horizons: village, tradition, and religion.

JIM: As far as we can tell, they don't have anything even remotely resembling what we would call goals.

RAYE: They believe in spirits, both good and bad, shamans, ancestor worship, herbal amulets, witch doctors, taboos, black magic, and animal sacrifice.

ACT TWO

JIM: Mostly chickens and ducks.

RAYE: They don't even know that other countries exist, except for Vietnam and China...maybe Laos. The weather is awful.

JIM: Noonday temperatures at Angkor Wat average 130 degrees; the cockroaches are as big as puppies and the bees are like sparrows.

RAYE: They have a jungle snake called two step: it bites you...you take two steps...

JIM: And then you die.

RAYE: Sooner or later everyone gets the Cambodian canter.

JIM: That's the local dysentery.

(Slides of Sihanouk in various guises)

RAYE: Now pretty much everyone supports Sihanouk. He's been here since 1952. The peasants adore him...call him Royal Father. His name in Sanskrit literally means Lion Hearted.

JIM: We just call him Snookie.

RAYE: By our standard he's a pretty pathetic leader—chases after women...been married six times, not all legal....

JIM: Fourteen children.

RAYE: His current favorite wife is Monique.

JIM: A beauty contest winner.

RAYE: Got his own gambling casino, palace soccer, basketball and volleyball teams. Plays the saxophone.

JIM: Even had a hit song, on the radio.

RAYE: Makes feature movies starring his favorite daughter, Bopha Devi. She's been married four times.

Puts General Tioulang, Minister of Foreign Affairs, and some of his other generals in walk-on parts.

JIM: Been known to use the country's entire armed forces helicopters in these movies.

RAYE: A real wild hair for us is that he consults a palace astrologer before making decisions on affairs of state.

Our job here is to convince the soldiers that their leaders are fighting for Peking, the monks, that the middle class hates them. And the middle class, that Sihanouk's neutralism is hurting the import-export business.

JIM: Cambodians are different than we are.

RAYE: For example, take anger...never show anger in front of them. Even the word for anger in their language is synonymous with madness.

Be polite. Eat whatever's offered to you, even if it's not appetizing.

JIM: Praise Buddhism and the monks.

RAYE: Don't dwell on past weaknesses; stick with the glories of the past, like Angkor Wat. Finally, Cambodians are jolly people.

JIM: They love silly jokes....

RAYE: But they don't get jokes about incomes taxes or Texas.

(The company, with the puppets, in Asian accents to the audience)

JOSIE: I went by boat to Thailand.

DANA: I hid in the jungle and lived there.

ROSALIND: I had a Christian sponsor who brought me to Minnesota.

ABE: I was homesick.

ACT TWO

JESSICA: I stayed inside and watched the snow and cried.

JOSIE: Sometimes the ancestors demand a sacrifice, a chicken or a pig.

JESSE: The neighbors call the police.

GEORGE: My suffering and anger keep me going.

PAMELA: It's not safe here. I'm afraid to watch the evening news.

ALMA: I don't want to know what's happening.

ROSALIND: I'm afraid to go out in my car. They might attack you at any time.

DANA: I thought as I grew older, I would forget.

ROSALIND: In the refugee camp they teach you how to flush the toilet, use the vacuum cleaner, and go to the post office.

GEORGE: I can't learn English.

(*Movie of war in Central America. To Sid Vicious, "My Way". ABE enters, dressed as a middle-class Central American.*)

ABE: The capucha is a hood made of rubber, which has a kind of tie at the end. This is what you do.... You put the hood over the person's head, and you tighten the strings so that no air can enter, then you tie his hands and ankles from behind, and you put him face down on the floor and row him back and forth...while someone else is tightening the strings on the hood.

What happens? He starts to lose consciousness...and just when he is about to faint...you jump on him, throw cold water on his face, or you slap him.

Then you interrogate him. If he says he doesn't know anything, you put the hood back on. Some will talk to save their lives. They invent just about anything.

There are those who are very macho and don't speak.

Sometimes we put Gamezon, an insecticide, inside their hood. It's very effective — burns the nose and eyes. People can't take it. They feel like they're dying. Torture is funny, some people can't take it. They just die.

You see their bodies by the roadside, ten kilometers from the city, hands tied behind them. They were the ones who couldn't take it.

A GLOSSARY

(Music: David Byrne and Brian Eno's "Mountain of Needles". Each woman lights a candle behind the china silk. Their faces are beautiful. Their voices are miked, serene and composed. The men move with the puppets in a kind of slow dream dance.)

JESSICA: ATROCITY, an unusually cruel act of brutality, totally outside all accepted standards of behavior.

PAMELA: AUTOGENOCIDE, the purposeful extermination of a race by its own members.

ROSALIND: BOAT PEOPLE, those who escaped since 1979 by sea.

ALMA: COYOTE, illegal alien smuggler.

JOSIE: DESAPARECIDO, to be disappeared, it refers to the many who are kidnapped and disappear in Central and Latin America.

PAMELA: EL PLAYON, a well-known location outside of San Salvador where the bodies of torture victims are left.

ACT TWO 55

ROSALIND: MANO BLANCO, the white hand, sign of warning of execution left by right-wing death squads in Central America.

ALMA: MOJADOS, the wet ones, those who cross the United States/Mexico border illegally.

JOSIE: OREJA, literally ear, government informers in Guatemala.

JESSICA: REFUGEE, any person who is outside his country of residence and who is unable and unwilling to avail himself of the protection of that country because of persecution of race or religion, or nationality.

ROSALIND: TUOL SENG, means hill of the poison tree, former high school in Phnom Penh used by the Khmer Rouge as an extermination center.

JOSIE: TORTURE, any act by which severe pain or suffering, whether physical or mental, is intentionally inflicted on a person for such purposes as obtaining from him information or confession.

(Blackout as the women blow out the candles.)

TESTIMONY

(A flame is projected on the scrim. In downstage lights, the following group is stuffing a large rag doll. The actors are body miked. They speak in urgent whispers.)

JESSE: They took us off the bus and questioned us. I was about to get back on the bus when they grabbed me and threw me in the back of a car and started to beat me up.

JOSIE: He was disappeared my husband and later appeared dead. On August 13th: The National Guard came to my house and picked me up.

JESSICA: I was with them...Los Indios. We ran for six hours. I saw people with their heads smashed open, their hands ripped off, their arms and legs were dangling.

(Loud crash off-stage. The actors look up matter-of-factly.)

JESSE: They took off all my clothes and when I was naked they poured water on my body and then they put me in an air-conditioned room.

ALMA: My brother...he was only fourteen years old... they cut off his tongue.... I saw this with my own eyes. They poured gasoline on him and they set him on fire. They made us watch...they said so we would not help the guerrillas.

JESSE: Then they put my head under water, in the bañera, and I started to drown.

(Crash)

JOSIE: They applied electric shock to my nostrils, my breasts, my vagina...and in my mouth and on my feet.

ALMA: They made us all watch.

VOICE: *(On tape)* You didn't have any food for ten days.

RAFAEL: *(On tape)* Sí, I didn't have any food for ten days.

JESSICA: I lost all sense of time.

JESSE: I knew I was going to die.

JOSIE: It was a life out of this world.

ALMA: They wouldn't let me sleep.

(Crash)

JESSE: They told me they would rape my little daughter in front of me.

ACT TWO

JESSICA: How the blood ran. They cut open his chest with a machete and he was still alive. He died in agony. They said they would come back for the others.

ALMA: Little baby Augusto's fingernails were missing. The soles of his feet were burned.

(Crash)

JESSE: I heard the others screaming. I realized it was the sound of my own torture.

JOSIE: They used the capucha.

ALMA: They found me. I was raped by seven men. I was shot in the leg. Look, here is the bullet hole. *(Holds up doll)* Yes, and then they put burning cigarettes on my legs. After I was in prison for five months, they took me out and left me naked in Apapa.

VOICE: *(On tape)* What is the airplane?

JAIME AND RAFAEL: *(On tape)* They take a person by the arm and leg...uhah...and then they turn them around and then they smash them against the wall.

(Crash)

VOICE: *(On tape)* What is the blender?

JAIME AND RAFAEL: *(On tape)* I am standing in the middle of the room nude and they turn me around so many times, and that along with beating me.

JESSE: When I got out of prison I hid in my sister's house; but then the death squad said they would kill me. So I hid again.

VOICE: *(On tape)* Do you think it would be dangerous for you if you were deported?

PAUL: *(On tape)* Sí. Claro que sí.

(The group has finished its work. They rise, sticking their sewing needles into the doll, and exit — all except ALMA,

who stands, holding the limp doll in her arms. She wraps it carefully in a fragment of the china silk.)

ALMA: In Spanish he whispers there is no time left.
It is the sound of scythes arcing in the wheat.
The ache of some field song in Salvador.
The wind along the prison, cautious
as Francisco's hand on the inside, touching
the walls as he walks. It is his wife's breath
slipping into his cell each night while he
imagines his hand to be hers. It is a small country.
There is nothing left that one man will not do to
another. (ALMA *leaves the doll on the chair.)*

DEAD LETTERS

(The stage is quite dark.)

ABE: To Lidia del Cid:
 I am on the brink between life and death because they accuse me of being a guerilla. Lidia, please don't cry.
I am not the first or the last such case in this world; after awhile, you come to realize anything can happen. I am very sad because I think only of death, of you and my children, and the mother I will never hug again. A kiss for them all. Treat them well. Put David to work and take care of María, as well as Marta, Juanita, and José Armandito. Give them all your love, because they will not have a father any longer. Only God's will can save me now.
 In my savings account in the factory, I have 901 quetzales. Take it out. I also owe Joaquín Mendez 126 quetzales. Use our savings and ask the union people to help you with all of this.
 There are no more words from your husband who has loved you so much with all his heart and soul. Please face life like a real woman.

ACT TWO

Take care of my children.
You are not the first woman in the world to become a widow.
Goodbye forever.
Cristóbal Armando Barrientos Mendoza.

JOSIE: He was a victim of spirits.

ROSALIND: What spirits?

JIM: Spirits of this country.

JESSICA: Last night when he died, he was watching *The Incredible Hulk.*

DANA: *(As* MARSHALL KY. *He is broken and distracted. He pauses, looking for words.)* So much lost...so many misunderstandings. American college kids used to call me a war monger. Now, my daughter listens to the U-2.
    I remember...we had our Camp David, too. A magnificent white villa on the beach. Kissinger came to lunch. He really knew how to use chopsticks.
    Some of us worked hard to be good leaders, to win the war against communism. Maybe we tried too hard to impress the Americans. We wanted them to like us...they were so tall.
    I remember the Honolulu Conference...everyone was there...McNamara, Rusk, Westmoreland...everyone.
    I gave a great speech about social justice and self government. Afterwards, Johnson said, "Boy, you talk just like an American."

(PAMELA *and* JESSICA *walk across the stage as Buddha exits.)*

PAMELA: It was this tiny puddle of fettucini with a wad of goat cheese on top. Are they making a movie here?

JESSICA: It's a miniseries. Richard Chamberlain is playing Ho Chi Minh.

PAMELA: She hasn't been outside without sunscreen since she was fourteen.

JESSICA: It's the only spa I know that gives you tiny electric shocks after the camomile herbal wrap.

PAMELA: Why?

JESSICA: Cellulite.

(Slides of water surfaces)

ROSALIND: Dear Mama and Papa,
   I would like to say to you, I love you very much. I'll never forget your faces in my life. I'll die lonely. Don't give me your tears, but your heart. When I die you won't be here and no one will stand next to me.
   Oh Papa and Mama. It's raining and I'm crying again. Before I die I want to have wings and fly back to see you and my lovely country. Mama, hold me in your arms and sing a song just as when I was little. Oh my heart will stop working, Mama and Papa, my country, my friends, please wait for me. I'll come back.
   At last this man died calmly. No one knew him. There were no tears for him.
   NGO THI BICH LE.

DYING IN YOUR DREAMS

(Music: Sankhala, modern gamelan music. This is a dream sequence.)

TAPE: The dead intervene at every moment of the living; the souls guide them, direct them, protect them, assist them with their eyes, which cut through the secret of life and death. The souls live in their memory, in their thoughts, in their dreams of a life

ACT TWO

still more intense than this earthly life. The cult of the dead is
the cult of memory.

(Puppets slowly dance in the ghostly light.)

ROSALIND: *(Lights a candle)* Yong Shua's mother had a dream:
Someone was taking my son away.
I followed them to the river.
They crossed to the other side in a boat.
My son was speaking another language and disappearing into the distance.

JIM: *(Lighting candle)* Bunphan had a dream.
The next day she felt a ghost in their new house.
Her husband Srisomphon noticed a strong smell of decay in the garden.
The next morning, he was dead on the bottom of the stairs.
His head was resting on a pillow.

JOSIE: *(Lighting candle)* Chang Yang had a dream.
Four huge demons came to take him away.
He begged them to allow him to say goodbye to his family and they refused.
Then, as he sat, watching the leaves turn to gold and fall from the trees, he gradually began to forget his loved ones.

(Blackout)

(Piercing music from the bamboo flute)

(The following lines are whispered in the black.)

ALL WOMEN: He was a victim of spirits.

ALL MEN: What spirits?

ALL WOMEN: Spirits of this country.

WAITING

(Loud crash)

(Projection: Ellis Island window shatters. Lights. Music: Paul Simon's "America". All move toward benches and wait for a bus, standing or sitting.)

(Tape: Voices during music)

TAPE: Introducing the first family cereal that's deliciously sweetened without sugar.
   Should you invest in an appliance service contract?
   Will estrogen keep you young?
   Cooking in the West Coast way.

(Music ends. Company rises for the bus. Freezes. Very slow light fade. The Golden Door brightens and then extinguishes. Black.)

END OF PLAY